Level Up:

Healing Mode Activated

You Took the Hit—

Now It's Time to Heal

by

Rick Morris

Disclaimer

The information contained in this book is intended to serve as a guide for parents dealing with children who have been affected by sexual abuse. While every effort has been made to ensure the accuracy and reliability of the information provided, this book is not a substitute for professional legal or medical advice, diagnosis, or treatment.

Consult a qualified healthcare provider for diagnosis and treatment if your child is experiencing mental health issues or other medical conditions. A licensed mental health counselor or medical doctor should be consulted for a thorough evaluation and appropriate treatment plan tailored to your child's needs.

By reading this book, you acknowledge that it is not a substitute for professional advice. The author and publisher disclaim any liability arising directly or indirectly from using the information in this book.

First Edition, 2025

ISBN: Printed: 979-8-9987467-1-0

Youtube: @Tools4TeensandParents
www.sayhelp.net
www.tools4teens.net

Contents

A Note to Parents and Caregivers:

How to Use This Book

If you're reading this, your child has experienced something no boy ever should—sexual abuse. First, let us say: **we're so sorry this happened to him, and we're grateful he's not facing this alone.** This book was created specifically for boys ages 12–14 who have experienced sexual abuse and are now navigating the confusing emotional, physical, and relational challenges that follow.

It's written in a way that speaks *directly to boys*—with honesty, clarity, and even humor—because healing doesn't happen through sugarcoating. It happens when we create space for boys to understand what happened, feel what they feel, and begin to believe again in their worth and strength. This book doesn't just explain trauma—it helps your child reclaim power, name their emotions, and walk forward without shame.

How You Can Support Your Child with This Book:

- **Read alongside him (if he agrees).** Some boys prefer privacy, but others may benefit from reading with a parent or discussing chapters together. Let him take the lead. Respect his boundaries while making yourself available.
- **Don't rush the process.** Each chapter covers a deep topic—abuse, guilt, identity, coping, relationships, and more. Your child may want to pause, reflect, or revisit sections. That's normal.
- **Invite conversation without forcing it.** After a chapter, you might simply say, "Was there anything in that chapter that stood out to you?" or "How did that part feel to read?" If he says nothing, that's okay. Just keep the door open.
- **Use the language in the book.** The metaphors and humor are intentional, designed to connect with boys. Phrases like "healing is like respawning" or "your feelings are like 100 unread texts" help

- normalize what he's feeling. Use them when you can tell him you're trying to understand his world.
- **Validate his experience.** He may struggle with shame, confusion, or even anger. The most healing words you can offer are: *"I believe you," "It wasn't your fault,"* and *"I'm here for you no matter what."*
- **Seek professional help if needed.** This book can be an incredible tool, but it isn't therapy. If your child continues to struggle or if the content stirs up intense emotions, consider working with a licensed therapist who specializes in trauma and sexual abuse.

What This Book Is (and isn't):

This book is not a textbook, and it's not a checklist for recovery. It's a **guide**, a **companion**, and a **conversation starter**. It doesn't promise overnight healing—but it does help boys start telling their truth, naming their pain, and seeing themselves as worthy of respect, love, and a full life.

You don't have to be perfect to support your child. You just need to show up, listen more than you speak, and remind him, again and again, that **he is not broken, he is not alone, and he is deeply loved.**

Thank you for being here. Your willingness to walk alongside him is already making a difference.

Rick Morris

Chapter 1: Understanding What Happened to You

If You're Reading This...

If you're reading this, you're probably dealing with a lot of tough feelings, maybe confusion, anger, shame, sadness, or even feeling totally numb. You might not even be sure if what happened to you *counts* as sexual abuse. Or maybe you *know* something was wrong, but you don't know how to explain it. This chapter is here to help you figure out what sexual abuse is, how it affects your feelings, and why it messes with how you see yourself.

What Exactly Is Sexual Abuse?

Sexual abuse happens when someone does sexual things with you—or makes you do things—with pressure, tricks, or without your full understanding. It doesn't have to be physical force. It can be emotional pressure, threats, lies, or taking advantage of your trust.

If someone you trusted—like a brother, cousin, friend, coach, or adult—touched you sexually, made you touch them, showed you porn, took inappropriate photos, or made sexual comments, that's sexual abuse. It doesn't matter who they were. What they did was wrong.

Knowing this is a big first step toward healing.

Common Feelings After Abuse

After something like this, you might feel all kinds of things—ashamed, embarrassed, confused, or even like it was your fault. Listen closely: **it was not your fault.** Not even a little.

It doesn't matter what you did, said, or didn't do. The abuse happened because of *their* choices, not yours.

You might also feel weird or confused about your body's reactions. Sometimes your body reacts during abuse even if you didn't want it to. That's just biology. It doesn't mean you wanted it. It doesn't mean you're to blame. Understanding this helps take away some of the shame and confusion.

Why Is Abuse So Confusing?

Abuse is confusing because it usually comes from someone you trusted. That makes everything feel messed up—like your sense of safety just got yanked away. You might start questioning who you can trust or even how you see yourself.

Here's one way to think of it:
"Understanding trauma is like trying to fix your Wi-Fi when it keeps dropping. You know something's wrong, it's invisible, and it's *not* your fault—but it still messes everything up."

If you're a guy, this can feel even more confusing. Society tells guys we're supposed to be strong, in control, and not show weakness. Abuse can make you feel powerless or like you're not "man enough." But that's a lie. Real strength is facing what happened and dealing with it—not pretending it didn't affect you.

Naming What You Feel

A big part of healing is knowing how you feel. Sounds simple, but it's not always easy. You might be:

- **Angry** – at the abuser, yourself, or the world
- **Sad** – like something was stolen from you
- **Ashamed or guilty** – worried people will see you differently
- **Anxious or afraid** – like it could happen again or someone might find out

These are normal reactions. You don't need to push them away. Naming them is a power move—it gives you back control.

You're Not Alone

You might feel like no one could possibly understand what you're going through. But the truth is, **a lot of other guys have been through this, too.** You're not weird. You're not broken. You're not the only one.

Talking to a therapist, teacher, coach, or adult you trust can help you feel less alone. Healing doesn't happen in silence—it happens with support.

Taking Back Your Power

What happened might've taken away your control. But you can start taking it back, one truth at a time:

- **You were sexually abused.**
- **It was not your fault.**
- **You're allowed to feel what you feel.**
- **You can get better.**

That's how healing begins—with honesty and courage.

"Your feelings after abuse are like a group chat with 100 unread messages—you don't know where to start, but ignoring it won't make it go away."

What's Coming Next

In the chapters ahead, you'll learn how to break the silence, deal with intense feelings, and rebuild your strength and confidence. There's no quick fix, but there *is* a path forward—and you're already on it.

Quote to Remember:

"You may not control all the events that happen to you, but you can decide not to be reduced by them."

— Maya Angelou

Chapter 2: Breaking the Silence

Talking about sexual abuse can feel scary, confusing, or even impossible. You might think, "No way I'm saying anything," and that's normal at first. But here's the truth: **speaking up is one of the most powerful things you can do to take your life back.** In this chapter, we'll talk about why it's so hard to tell someone, why it's important, and how using your voice makes you stronger, not weaker.

Why Is Speaking Out So Hard?

Keeping abuse a secret feels easier at first. You might worry about what people will say, how your family will react, or if anyone will even believe you. Some reasons it feels hard to talk are:

- **Fear of Not Being Believed**: You're scared people will think you're lying or making it up.
- **Feeling Embarrassed or Ashamed**: You might feel like the abuse was somehow your fault, even though it wasn't.
- **Fear of Getting Someone in Trouble**: You might not want to cause problems in your family or friendship circle.
- **Worry About Being Judged**: You might think people will look at you differently or treat you weird after they know.

These fears are real. But staying silent keeps the pain locked inside you, and that's not where it belongs. It belongs on the person who hurt you—not on you.

The Power of Telling Your Story

When you finally speak out—even just to one trusted person—you start taking back control. Here's why using your voice is powerful:

- **It lets you breathe again**. Holding a secret that heavy is exhausting.
- **It shows you're not alone**. People can support you once they know what you're dealing with.
- **It smashes shame**. Shame grows in silence. Telling someone punches shame right in the face.
- **It stops the cycle**. You might even protect someone else by speaking up.

Even if you just tell one person, that's a huge win. It doesn't have to be a public speech. It can be a whisper.

Who Should You Talk To?

Pick someone you feel safe with. Maybe it's:

- A counselor or therapist
- A parent, grandparent, or trusted family member
- A teacher or school counselor
- A coach or mentor

Not every adult gets it right the first time. If someone doesn't listen well or believe you, **don't give up**. Find someone who will.

When you're ready to talk, it can help to:

- **Write it down first**. Sometimes writing a letter is easier than saying it out loud.
- **Practice what you want to say**. It's okay to keep it simple: "I need to tell you something that happened to me. It's really hard to talk about."
- **Pick a calm, private time**. You deserve to feel safe when you speak.

How People Might React

Some people will feel sad. Some will feel angry—*for you*. Some might not know what to say at all. That's about **them**, not you.

The most important thing: **their reaction doesn't change the truth of what happened to you**.

If someone doesn't react the way you hoped, remember: you're still brave for telling your truth. You can always find someone else who will listen better.

Breaking Your Silence = Reclaiming Your Power

Think of it like this:

Keeping abuse a secret is like carrying a 500-pound backpack every day. Telling someone is like dropping that backpack at their feet and saying, "This isn't mine to carry anymore."

When you speak out, you're choosing healing over hiding. You're choosing yourself.

You are not responsible for other people's feelings about your story. You are responsible for protecting yourself and your future.

What's Next?

Once you break the silence, healing starts to move faster. You'll still have hard days, but you won't be alone anymore. You'll learn ways to deal with the emotions that come up, and you'll start to feel lighter inside.

The next chapters will help you understand that none of this was your fault, deal with tough feelings, and start rebuilding your strength.

You have a right to be heard. You deserve healing. And the first step is speaking your truth.

"No matter how dark the night, morning always comes. And our journey begins anew."

— Lulu, Final Fantasy X

Chapter 3: It Was Not Your Fault

If you've been blaming yourself for what happened, you're not alone. Most guys who go through sexual abuse think somehow they should've fought harder, said something sooner, or stopped it. But here's the truth you need to grab onto: **none of it was your fault. Not then. Not now. Not ever.**

Why You Might Feel Guilty

After abuse, it's normal to have questions spinning in your head like:

- "Why didn't I fight harder?"
- "Did I do something to cause it?"
- "If my body reacted, does that mean I wanted it?"

No. To all of that. Abuse isn't about what you did or didn't do—it's about the choices someone else made. They chose to hurt you. They crossed the line. They are 100% responsible for what happened.

Understanding Manipulation

Most abusers don't just attack out of nowhere. They manipulate you first. They might have:

- Made you feel special or chosen
- Threatened you to stay quiet
- Acted like what was happening was "normal" or "okay"

That's not your fault either. Being tricked or pressured by someone you trusted doesn't mean you agreed. It means they used their power in a messed-up way.

If you froze during the abuse, if you didn't scream or fight back, that's normal too. Your brain and body were trying to survive the best way they knew how.

Where the Shame Belongs

Feeling ashamed after abuse is super common. But the shame doesn't belong to you. Shame belongs 100% to the person who hurt you.

Imagine carrying around a heavy backpack full of someone else's garbage. That's what it's like holding onto shame that isn't yours. **It's time to drop that backpack.**

Physical Responses Don't Mean Consent

Sometimes your body reacts during abuse—like getting physically aroused—even when you didn't want it. That's just biology. It doesn't mean you liked it or asked for it. Your body's reactions don't erase the fact that you were hurt against your will.

The wrongness of what happened isn't about your body's reaction—it's about the choices someone else made without your permission.

You Didn't "Ask for It"

It doesn't matter:

- What you wore
- What you said
- If you trusted them
- If you froze and didn't fight
- If you were curious about sex

Nothing about you made it okay for someone to abuse you.

You didn't ask for it. Period.

Giving Back the Blame

It's powerful to mentally hand the blame back where it belongs. You can say in your mind or out loud:

- "They chose to hurt me."
- "It's not my shame to carry."
- "I'm not responsible for what they did."

You survived something hard. That makes you strong—not guilty.

Ways to Deal With Guilt and Shame

Here are a few ways to start shaking off guilt:

- **Positive Self-Talk**: Catch yourself when you start blaming yourself and replace it with the truth: *"It wasn't my fault."*
- **Talk to Someone Safe**: Telling a counselor or trusted adult how you're feeling can help lift the weight off your chest.

- **Write It Down**: Sometimes writing a letter you never send—getting all your angry or guilty thoughts out—can help you let go.

Learning Self-Compassion

You deserve the same kindness you'd give a friend who went through something awful. Self-compassion means saying:

- "I deserved better."
- "It's okay to still feel hurt."
- "Healing takes time, and I'm worth it."

You might have to remind yourself of these things every single day. That's not weakness. That's how healing works.

Moving Forward

Accepting that the abuse wasn't your fault is like cutting a heavy chain off your ankle. It won't fix everything instantly, but it gives you the freedom to move forward.

You are not your trauma. You are not your guilt. You are not your shame.

You are a survivor, and you deserve a future full of strength, respect, and peace.

Get up, you're not done yet."

— *Apex Legends*

Chapter 4: How Abuse Affects Your Identity and Masculinity

Sexual abuse doesn't just hurt your body—it messes with how you see yourself. It can make you feel confused about who you are, what it means to be strong, and how you fit into the world. If you've ever felt like you're not "man enough" because of what happened, you're not alone. But here's the truth: **abuse doesn't change your worth. It doesn't change your masculinity. It doesn't define you.**

Why Abuse Creates Confusion About Masculinity

Growing up, you've probably heard a lot of ideas about what it means to "be a man." Stuff like:

- "Be tough."
- "Don't cry."
- "Always be in control."
- "Handle everything by yourself."

When something bad like abuse happens, it smashes into those ideas. You might start thinking:

- "Am I weak because I didn't stop it?"
- "Does this make me different from other guys?"
- "Am I less of a man now?"

The answer to all of that is **NO**.

Getting hurt doesn't make you weak. Speaking up, getting help, and healing? **That's real strength.**

Busting Myths About Masculinity

Here are some lies you might have heard—and the truth you need to hold onto:

- **Lie:** Real men don't get hurt.
  Truth: Everyone can get hurt. Surviving pain takes guts.
- **Lie:** Showing emotion makes you weak.
  Truth: Being able to cry, ask for help, or admit you're scared takes massive strength.
- **Lie:** You have to prove you're "man enough" through sex or toughness.
  Truth: Being a real man is about respect—respect for yourself and others.

You don't have to live by anyone else's broken rules about what makes you valuable.

How Abuse Hits Your Self-Worth

After abuse, it's easy to feel:

- Like you're "damaged goods."
- Like nobody would respect you if they knew the truth.
- Like you're carrying something ugly inside you.

Those feelings are real—but **they're wrong**.

What someone did to you doesn't change your worth. It doesn't make you less important. It doesn't erase your right to be proud of who you are.

Your true value is bigger than anything someone else ever did to you.

Rebuilding How You See Yourself

You get to rebuild your identity the way you want—not based on what happened to you. Here's how to start:

- **Do stuff you love.** Sports, gaming, music, art—whatever reminds you who you are outside of the abuse.
- **Hang out with people who lift you up.** Stick with friends, family, or mentors who make you feel respected and safe.
- **Speak truth over yourself.** Say it out loud if you have to: *"I am strong. I am enough. I am rebuilding."*

Every time you treat yourself with kindness and respect, you prove to yourself that you're more powerful than what hurt you.

Redefining Masculinity On Your Terms

You don't have to copy someone else's version of what "being a man" means. You can decide for yourself.

Real masculinity is about:

- Respecting yourself and others
- Being honest about how you feel
- Standing up for what's right
- Protecting people who are vulnerable
- Living with courage, even when you're scared

It's not about being the toughest guy in the room—it's about being the realest guy in the room.

You are already enough. You were enough the whole time.

Final Thoughts

The abuse you survived doesn't get to tell you who you are.
You do.

Your strength isn't measured by how much you hide your pain. It's measured by how bravely you face it.

The chapters ahead will keep helping you build that strength—emotionally, physically, and mentally.

"It's not what you call me, it's what I answer to."

— African Proverb

Chapter 5: Unhealthy Coping: Why Acting Out Doesn't Help

After something bad happens—like being sexually abused—it's normal to want to do *anything* to not feel the pain. Sometimes that means making choices that seem like they help for a minute but actually make things worse. These are called unhealthy coping strategies. They might feel good for a little bit, but they don't heal you. They just pile more junk on top of the hurt.

Why Do Guys Act Out After Abuse?

When you're carrying a ton of anger, sadness, confusion, or shame, it feels like you're going to explode if you don't do something. So you might:

- Take risks like fighting, stealing, or using substances
- Act out sexually, trying to feel in control or powerful again
- Constantly chase attention from girls, guys, or anyone
- Try to feel "normal" by doing dangerous stuff

At first, these things might give you a rush or make you feel better. But it never lasts. It's like putting duct tape over a cracked phone screen—it doesn't really fix anything.

Why Acting Out Doesn't Heal You

Here's the thing about unhealthy coping: it covers up your pain instead of helping you deal with it. It tricks you into feeling like you're strong, when really, you're just burying the wound deeper.

Problems with acting out:

- You stay stuck feeling empty and angry inside.
- You get yourself into even bigger messes (health problems, legal trouble, broken relationships).
- You start believing lies about yourself, like you're worthless or out of control.

The truth is, real healing isn't about pretending you're fine. It's about facing your hurt in a way that actually helps you heal long-term.

How to Know if You're Coping Unhealthily

Ask yourself:

- Am I doing this to feel better for a few minutes—or because it's good for me long-term?
- Am I trying to prove something to other people?
- Do I feel worse afterward?

If the answer is "yeah," it's probably not a healthy way to deal.

Better Ways to Cope That Actually Help

You don’t have to fake it. You don't have to destroy yourself to feel powerful again. There are real ways to deal with the hurt that actually make you stronger:

- **Talk to someone you trust.** Keeping everything inside just makes the pressure worse.
- **Move your body.** Sports, working out, walking, whatever—physical movement helps clear out stress.
- **Create something.** Art, music, writing, gaming builds, whatever helps you *make* instead of *break*.
- **Breathe and chill.** Try deep breathing, mindfulness, or just being outside.
- **Set small goals.** Winning little battles builds real confidence—not fake rushes.

Choosing healthy ways to cope isn’t weakness. It’s strategy. It’s playing the long game instead of rage-quitting your own life.

Reclaiming Your Power

Every time you choose a healthy way to deal with pain, you're flipping the script. You're proving you're in charge—not the abuse, not the pain, not the bad memories.

Healing isn't about pretending you're fine. It's about being real, facing the hard stuff, and building a life where you're in control—not your trauma.

You're not here to self-destruct.
You're here to heal, rebuild, and **level up**.

"No matter who you are, where you're from, your skin color, or your gender identity — speak yourself."

— RM (BTS)

Chapter 6: Building Healthy Relationships After Abuse

When someone you trusted hurts you, it can mess up how you see everybody. You might start thinking, "I can't trust anyone" or "Everyone's just waiting to hurt me." It makes sense if you feel that way. But the truth is, **not everyone will betray you.** There are good people out there—and you deserve to find them.

This chapter is about how to spot healthy relationships, rebuild trust, and protect yourself without shutting down completely.

Why Relationships Feel So Hard

After being abused, you might:

- Feel scared to get close to anyone
- Worry that if you trust again, you'll just get hurt
- Feel like you have to be on guard 24/7
- Get uncomfortable even when someone is just being nice

Those feelings are totally normal. But if you stay locked behind your walls forever, it's like living in a castle with no door—you're safe, but you're also stuck. Healing means learning how to open the door carefully, not knocking down all your defenses at once.

What Healthy Relationships Actually Look Like

Here's the cheat code: **Healthy people don't make you feel small, unsafe, or confused.**

Healthy relationships have:

- **Respect**: They listen to you and care about your feelings.
- **Trust**: You don't have to guess if they're lying or using you.
- **Good Communication**: You can talk openly—even about tough stuff.
- **Support**: They lift you up, not tear you down.
- **Boundaries**: They don't push you to do things you're not ready for.

If someone acts shady, ignores your feelings, or pressures you—**that's a red flag.** You don't owe anyone your time, attention, or loyalty if they don't treat you right.

How to Rebuild Trust Safely

Rebuilding trust is like rebuilding a bridge—you do it *one plank at a time*, not all at once.

- **Start Small**: Share little things first. See how they handle it.
- **Pay Attention**: Watch if their actions match their words.
- **Trust Your Gut**: If something feels off, it probably is.
- **Go Slow**: You get to set the pace. Real friends won't rush you.

You're allowed to take your time. Trust isn't something you give away for free—it's something people earn by treating you right over and over.

How to Set Boundaries (And Stick to Them)

Boundaries are like your personal rules for what's okay and what's not. Setting boundaries shows you respect yourself. Here's how:

- **Be clear**: "I don't like being touched like that." / "I'm not ready to talk about that."
- **Stick to it**: If they keep pushing, step away. Respect is non-negotiable.
- **No excuses**: If someone disrespects your boundary once, it's a warning. If they do it again, it's time to bounce.

You have the right to say NO without feeling guilty. You have the right to protect your space and your feelings.

What About Dating?

If you're thinking about dating or being close with someone someday, it's normal to feel freaked out. Abuse can leave scars around touch, trust, and intimacy. Here's what matters:

- **Take it slow**: You don't owe anyone romance, touch, or attention just because they like you.
- **Communicate clearly**: A healthy relationship is built on honesty, not games.
- **Prioritize respect**: If they don't respect your boundaries, it's not love.

The right person will understand and honor your healing journey. You won't have to explain your entire past for them to be patient and kind.

When Relationships Feel Overwhelming

Sometimes even good relationships feel scary after abuse. If you notice:

- You're panicking over small stuff
- You're feeling angry for no clear reason
- You want to run away or hide

Take a breath. Step back if you need to. Talk to someone you trust about it—a therapist, mentor, or a real friend. Healing isn't about being perfect. It's about noticing what you feel and taking care of yourself first.

Final Thoughts

Healing doesn't mean you trust everybody.
It means you learn to trust the *right* people.

You deserve friendships and relationships that are built on real respect, honesty, and safety. No rushing. No pressure. No games.

You deserve to build a life full of people who lift you up—not weigh you down.

"The people you surround yourself with can either lift you higher or drag you down. Choose wisely."

— Unknown

Chapter 7: Taking Control of Your Emotions

After being abused, your emotions can feel like they're running the show. One minute you're fine, the next minute you're angry, anxious, sad, or just numb. It can feel like you have no control. But here's the good news: **you can learn to take your emotions off "boss mode" and put yourself back in charge.**

You don't have to let feelings wreck your day, your friendships, or your future. You can learn to handle them like a boss.

Why Emotions Feel So Out of Control

Trauma messes with your brain and body. It's like your emotional "alarm system" got broken—sometimes it goes off too much, sometimes not enough.

You might notice:

- You snap at people without meaning to
- You get super anxious or can't sit still
- You feel totally frozen or zoned out
- You get sad and have no idea why

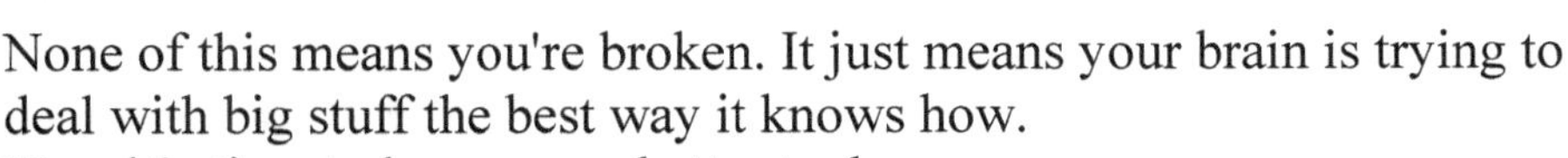

None of this means you're broken. It just means your brain is trying to deal with big stuff the best way it knows how.
Now it's time to learn some better tools.

How to Handle Anger Without Exploding

Anger after abuse is normal. It's okay to be mad—it's what you do with that anger that matters.

Ways to deal with anger safely:

- **Move your body**: Run, hit a punching bag, shoot hoops, do push-ups—get that energy out!
- **Write it out**: Journal your anger. You don't have to show it to anyone.
- **Breathe before you react**: When you feel yourself boiling, count slowly to 10 while breathing deep.

Important: Anger is a feeling. Hurting people, breaking stuff, or hurting yourself because you're angry is a choice—and it's not the one that helps you heal.

How to Handle Anxiety Without Panicking

Anxiety after abuse is like your brain hitting the "danger" button even when you're safe now.

Ways to deal with anxiety:

- **Ground yourself**: Look around and name 5 things you can see, 4 things you can touch, 3 things you hear, 2 things you smell, 1 thing you taste.
- **Breathe**: Inhale for 4 seconds, hold for 4, exhale for 4. Repeat until your heart slows down.
- **Focus on NOW**: Worry is usually about the past or future. Remind yourself, *"Right now, I am okay."*

How to Handle Sadness Without Drowning In It

Sadness after abuse hits deep. You're grieving the loss of trust, safety, and maybe even who you thought you were before.

Ways to deal with sadness:

- **Talk it out**: Find a therapist, counselor, or someone you trust. Sadness shrinks when you share it.
- **Stay active**: Moving your body helps your mind, even if you don't feel like it.
- **Do one thing you enjoy every day**: Even something small, like gaming for a bit, listening to music, or getting outside.

You don't have to be happy all the time. You just need to keep moving forward, even when it's hard.

Building Emotional Strength (AKA Resilience)

Resilience is like emotional armor. It doesn't mean you never get hurt, it means you know how to get back up.

Ways to build resilience:

- **Positive self-talk**: Say stuff like, *"I'm strong enough to get through this,"* even when you don't totally believe it yet.
- **Set small goals**: Winning little battles builds real strength.
- **Ask for help**: Real strength is knowing when to reach out, not trying to do it all alone.

Finding Healthy Outlets

Sometimes emotions are too big to just "think away." You need real ways to let them out safely:

- Play sports
- Create music, art, or writing
- Hang out with friends who make you laugh
- Spend time outside
- Learn deep breathing or mindfulness exercises

You're not weak for needing outlets. You're smart for giving yourself tools that work.

Final Thoughts

Taking control of your emotions doesn't mean pretending bad stuff never happened.
It means learning how to face what you feel, deal with it in smart ways, and stay in control of your life—not just your reactions.

Every time you handle a tough feeling in a healthy way, you're building the life you deserve—one choice at a time.

"It's not who I am underneath, but what I do that defines me."

— Batman (Christian Bale)

Chapter 8: Healing Your Body and Mind

When you've been through something like sexual abuse, healing isn't just about feeling better emotionally—it's about reconnecting with your body too. Trauma can make you feel like your mind and your body are on two different teams. You might even feel disconnected, angry at your body, or like you can't trust it anymore. Healing means getting your body and mind back on the same side.

This chapter will show you how to start rebuilding trust with yourself from the inside out.

How Trauma Messes with Your Body

Even when the abuse is over, your body remembers. Sometimes it shows up as:

- Tension in your shoulders, neck, or jaw
- Headaches, stomach aches, or random pains
- Trouble sleeping or nightmares
- Feeling tired all the time
- Feeling numb or like you're watching your life from outside your body

None of these things mean you're broken. It just means your body needs some attention and care too.

Taking Care of Your Physical Health

A strong body helps build a strong mind. Here are some simple ways to start healing physically:

- **Move Your Body**: You don't have to become a pro athlete. Walk, skate, bike, dance, lift weights, whatever gets you moving and burns off stress.
- **Eat to Fuel, Not Punish**: Try to eat real food—fruits, veggies, proteins. You don't have to be perfect, just aim to fuel yourself instead of junk-loading every day.
- **Prioritize Sleep**: Create a routine: shut off screens an hour before bed, listen to music, or read something chill. Your body heals best when you're resting.
- **Drink Water**: Staying hydrated helps your mood, your energy, and your brain.

Taking care of your body isn't about looks. It's about giving yourself the strength to heal.

Taking Care of Your Emotional Health

Your mind needs care just like your body does. Here's how:

- **Let Yourself Feel**: It's okay to feel sad, mad, scared, or even numb. Emotions are part of healing. Don't shove them down.
- **Write It Out**: Journaling helps clear out the emotional junk bouncing around in your head.
- **Talk to Someone**: Therapy, counseling, or a trusted adult gives you a safe space to unload.

- **Practice Mindfulness**: Simple breathing exercises or just paying attention to what's around you can help keep anxiety from running wild.

Reconnect With Your Body in a Positive Way

When you've been abused, sometimes your body doesn't feel like "yours" anymore. Healing means taking back your space inside your own skin.

Ways to reconnect with your body:

- **Do things that make you feel alive**: Swimming, climbing, hiking, dancing—whatever reminds you that your body is capable and strong.
- **Set boundaries**: It's okay to say "I don't want to be hugged" or "I need more space." You're allowed to protect your physical space.
- **Use positive self-talk**: Instead of saying, "My body is broken," say, "My body is healing."

Your body isn't the enemy. It's your teammate in getting your life back.

Be Patient With the Process

Healing isn't like flipping a light switch. It's more like leveling up in a game—it takes time, practice, and a lot of do-overs. Some days will feel strong. Some days will feel like you're starting from zero again. That's normal.

The key is **not giving up on yourself.** Keep showing up. Keep taking small steps. They add up.

Final Thoughts

Your mind and your body are on your side. Healing means taking care of both, treating yourself with respect, and giving yourself the time and space you need to get stronger.

You deserve a life where your body feels safe again and your mind feels clear again. And it's absolutely possible—you're already doing it by choosing to heal.

"I've failed over and over again in my life. And that is why I succeed."

— Michael Jordan

Chapter 9: Empowering Yourself and Rediscovering Your Strength

When someone abuses you, it can feel like they took something you can never get back—your power, your confidence, your sense of who you are. But here's what's real: **they don't get the final say about your life. You do.**

You are way stronger than what happened to you. This chapter is about finding that strength again and building the life you deserve.

What Real Strength Looks Like

Maybe people told you before that being strong means:

- Never crying
- Never asking for help
- Always acting tough
- Pretending you're fine even when you're not

That's garbage.

Real strength looks like:

- Facing hard feelings instead of hiding them
- Asking for support when you need it
- Setting boundaries even when it's uncomfortable
- Choosing to heal instead of staying stuck

Strength isn't about pretending nothing bothers you. It's about standing back up after you've been knocked down.

Abuse tries to destroy your confidence. But you can rebuild it, step by step.

Ways to rebuild confidence:

- **Challenge negative thoughts**: When you catch yourself thinking "I'm weak" or "I'm broken," stop and correct it: *"I'm strong because I survived."*
- **Set small goals and crush them**: Start small—like working out a few days a week, finishing a project, speaking up when something's wrong. Every win counts.

- **Take care of how you present yourself**: Shower, clean clothes, take pride in how you show up for yourself.
- **Choose positive people**: Hang out with people who lift you up, not tear you down.

Confidence isn't something you either "have" or "don't have." It's something you build—and you're already building it by being here.

Creating a Healthy Self-Image

Sometimes abuse leaves you feeling ugly, weak, or worthless. Those thoughts are lies. They're leftover junk from what someone else did to you.

Start changing your self-image by:

- **Focusing on what your body can do**, not just how it looks
- **Not comparing yourself to others**—social media shows everyone's "highlight reel," not their real struggles

- **Talking to yourself like you would talk to your best friend**—with encouragement, patience, and respect

You don't have to look perfect, act perfect, or be perfect.
You just have to keep showing up for yourself.

Redefining Masculinity

You don't have to live by anybody else's version of what being a "man" means. You get to define it for yourself.

Healthy masculinity looks like:

- Being honest about your emotions
- Respecting yourself and others
- Standing up for people who need it
- Setting and respecting boundaries
- Living with courage and kindness

It's not about "acting tough." It's about being true to yourself.

Turning Your Pain into Power

What happened to you sucked. It was wrong. But it doesn't have to be the end of your story.

You can take what you've been through and use it to:

- Help others who are hurting
- Set an example of resilience
- Build a life that's bigger and stronger than what tried to break you

Pain doesn't define you. How you rise from it does.

Final Thoughts

The abuse you survived does not get to be the headline of your life.
You are not a victim.
You are not broken.
You are **strong**, **wise**, and **powerful beyond measure**.

Every time you choose healing over hiding, honesty over shame, and hope over despair, you're reclaiming your strength.

You're not just surviving anymore.
You're rising.

"Even Mario starts small. He just finds the right mushroom."

— *Internet quote*

Chapter 10: Moving Forward – Your New Beginning

You've already done something incredible—you made it through the hardest parts. You've faced the truth about what happened, you learned about your feelings, you figured out how to handle anger, fear, sadness, and shame. You started healing.

Now it's time for the next part of your journey: **moving forward.**

Moving forward doesn't mean forgetting. It means living with strength, pride, and purpose. It means creating a life that's bigger, brighter, and stronger than anything that tried to break you.

Healing is a Journey, Not a Straight Line

Some days you'll feel unstoppable. Other days, you might feel stuck, sad, or angry again. That's normal. Healing isn't a straight climb—it's more like leveling up in a tough video game. You'll mess up sometimes. You'll fall back sometimes.
But you keep moving.

If you fall down, get up. Every single time.

Your future isn't about having a "perfect" life. It's about building a life where you know your worth and never forget your strength.

Choosing the Right People

The people you surround yourself with matter more than you think. The right people:

- Respect your boundaries
- Support your dreams
- Believe in your healing
- Treat you like you matter

If someone puts you down, disrespects your healing, or acts toxic, you don't need them in your life. You deserve a crew that lifts you higher, not drags you down.

Keeping Healthy Habits Going

The skills you learned here—managing emotions, setting boundaries, speaking up—aren't just for right now. They're for life.

Keep practicing:

- Journaling or writing when your mind feels full
- Moving your body to shake off stress
- Breathing through anxiety or panic
- Talking to people who make you feel safe
- Setting goals that get you excited about the future

These tools are your armor. They'll help you keep healing no matter what life throws your way.

Setting Goals for Your Future

Your past doesn't control your future—you do.

Dream big. Start small. Some ideas:

- Crush school or career goals
- Build strong friendships and relationships
- Find hobbies or passions that make you feel alive
- Help other people who are struggling
- Become the kind of person you want to be

Every goal you chase is another step toward the life you deserve.

Writing Your Own Story

What happened to you will always be a part of your story—but it's not the whole story.
It's just a few rough chapters.
You are the author now.
You get to write the rest.

You get to decide who you want to be. You get to build a life that's full of strength, kindness, and hope.

The pain didn't win.
You did.

And every day you keep choosing yourself, you win again.

Final Thoughts

Your life matters.
Your dreams matter.
Your healing matters.

You survived something that could have crushed you—but you didn't let it.
You kept going.
You fought for your future.
And now, your next chapter can be anything you want it to be.

The sunrise is yours.
The future is yours.
And you are absolutely worth it.

"Every day is a chance to begin again."

— Buddha

Final Words from Me to You

If you made it this far, I want you to know something really important: **I'm proud of you.**

Writing this book wasn't easy for me, just like reading it probably wasn't easy for you. I wrote it because I know what it feels like to carry heavy stuff around—confusion, fear, anger, shame—and not know where to put it. I wanted you to have something I wish every hurting boy had: real answers, real hope, and real strength to move forward.

- *You are not alone.*
- *You are not broken.*
- *You are not defined by what someone else chose to do to you.*
- *You have a life ahead of you that's bigger and brighter than the pain behind you.*
- *You have the power to heal, to grow, and to build something better than you might even believe is possible right now.*

Every single day you choose healing over hiding, strength over silence, and hope over fear—you win. And even when it feels hard (because some days it will), you are still moving forward.

I hope someday we will live in a world where books like this aren't needed anymore.

But until then, know this:

You matter. Your story matters. Your future matters.

Keep going. Keep fighting for yourself. Keep becoming the strong, courageous, amazing man you were always meant to be.

I believe in you.

APPENDIX

Caregiver Cheat Sheet: Supporting Your Child Through Healing

Audience: Parents and caregivers of boys ages 12–14 who have experienced sexual abuse
Purpose: A quick-reference guide to help you support your child while using this book

---

 DOs: What Helps Most

Strategy	Why It Helps
Listen more than you talk	Your child needs space to process. Silence can be healing.
Validate feelings	Say things like, "That makes sense," or "It's okay to feel that way."
Reinforce: It wasn't your fault	Your child may carry guilt or shame. Repeating this truth matters.
Use book language	Using familiar metaphors helps your child feel understood (e.g., "glitch," "leveling up," "respawn").
Let your child set the pace	Healing isn't linear. Some days he'll want to talk; some days he won't.
Create a safe space	Be predictable, calm, and nonjudgmental. Emotional safety encourages disclosure.
Encourage breaks	Some chapters may hit hard. Let him pause when needed.
Seek professional help if needed	Books are helpful, but therapy can deepen healing and offer structured support.

DON'Ts: What to Avoid

Behavior	Why It's Harmful
Pushing for details	Asking, "What exactly happened?" can feel invasive and unsafe.
Minimizing the abuse	Phrases like "It could've been worse" or "At least..." can shut your child down.
Trying to fix everything	He doesn't need solutions—he needs support, presence, and belief.
Comparing experiences	Saying, "That happened to someone else too" may make him feel less unique or heard.
Making it about you	Keep the focus on his feelings. Process your emotions separately, with support.

Helpful Phrases to Say Often

- "I believe you."
- "You didn't deserve what happened."
- "I'm proud of you for being brave."
- "It's okay to feel confused/angry/sad."
- "You can talk to me anytime—or not. I'm here no matter what."
- "You are not broken. You are healing."

Key Concepts in the Book

Chapter Theme	Reminder for You
Understanding abuse	Kids may not fully recognize their experience as abuse. Help clarify without pressuring.
Breaking the silence	Let him lead. Praise the courage it takes to speak up.
It wasn't his fault	This truth may need to be repeated dozens of times. Keep saying it.
Identity & masculinity	Reassure him that being vulnerable and needing help is *not* weakness.
Coping & behavior	Understand that acting out may come from pain—not defiance. Offer healthier alternatives.
Emotional regulation	Model emotional control and teach calming strategies without shaming big emotions.
Healthy relationships	Reinforce consent, respect, and boundaries in your daily interactions.
Body connection	Promote positive body language and activities that rebuild connection (e.g., sports, yoga, nature).
Empowerment	Encourage hobbies, goals, and decisions that give him a sense of control.
Moving forward	Celebrate growth, not perfection. Focus on his strengths and progress.

What to Revisit Together

- Page through difficult chapters slowly over time
- Talk about favorite quotes or metaphors
- Reflect on the last chapter: *What has changed since then?*
- Ask: "What do you want your healing to look like?"

HEALING CHEAT SHEET FOR BOYS

Your Fast Guide to Understanding, Coping, and Moving Forward

The Big Truths

- **It was not your fault.** Period.
- **Your body's reactions don't mean you wanted it.**
- **You are not broken — you're healing.**
- **Real strength means facing hard stuff, not hiding it.**
- **You get to choose who you become next.**

Top Tips from Each Chapter

Chapter	What to Remember
1. What Happened to You	Abuse is when someone does sexual stuff you didn't want or understand. It's confusing — but you're not crazy.
2. Breaking the Silence	Telling your story is hard, but powerful. You don't have to shout it. Just don't keep it locked inside.
3. Not Your Fault	The shame, guilt, and blame? They belong to the person who hurt you — not you.
4. Identity & Masculinity	Being a guy doesn't mean being silent, tough, or numb. Real masculinity = honesty, respect, and courage.
5. Unhealthy Coping	Acting out might feel like control — but it doesn't heal you. Healing comes from facing the pain, not avoiding it.
6. Healthy Relationships	You deserve relationships with trust, boundaries, and respect. Learn to say no and mean it.
7. Handling Emotions	Anger, sadness, and fear are normal. Use tools like breathing, talking, or moving your body to handle them.
8. Body + Mind Healing	Taking care of your body (food, sleep, movement) helps your brain feel better too.
9. Rebuilding Strength	You're strong because you're still here. Set goals. Be kind to yourself. Stay in the fight.
10. Moving Forward	Healing takes time. Set goals. Choose your crew wisely. You write the next chapter — not your abuser.

When You Feel Confused or Triggered

- Pause and breathe: 4 in, 4 hold, 4 out
- Write it down in your phone notes or a journal
- Remind yourself: *"This moment is temporary. I've survived worse."*
- Talk to someone you trust — you don't have to do this alone.

Your Power Moves

- Say "no" when something feels wrong
- Speak up even if your voice shakes
- Be honest about your feelings
- Do something that makes you feel proud every week
- Remember: **You didn't choose what happened to you, but you DO get to choose what happens next.**

"You are not what happened to you. You are what you choose to become."
— *Carl Jung*

"Your feelings are like a group chat with 100 unread messages. It's messy — but you've got to start somewhere."
— *From this book*

WORKBOOK PAGES FOR YOUR HEALING JOURNEY

1. My Truths Page

(Affirmation & Identity Clarification)

Complete the sentences below. You can come back to this page anytime.

What happened to me was:	
It was **not** my fault because:	
I want to remember that I am:	
I'm strong because:	
I'm allowed to feel:	
My past doesn't define me. I define me.	

2. Emotion Check-In Tracker

(Daily emotional awareness practice)

Today I feel (circle any):

Angry Sad Numb Anxious

Calm Confused Hopeful

Why do I think I feel this way?

What do I need right now to feel better or safe?

One thing I'm proud of today:

Repeat this daily or when emotions feel too big.

---

3. Triggers and Safety Plan

(For identifying what sets them off & how to handle it)

Stuff that makes me feel unsafe or freaked out (triggers):

- ____________________
- ____________________
- ____________________

What I can do when I feel triggered:

- [x] Leave the situation
- [x] Breathe slowly
- [x] Text/call someone safe
- [x] Journal or draw
- [x] Remind myself: "I'm safe now."

People I trust and can talk to:

1. ____________________
2. ____________________
3. ____________________

4. Practice Saying No and Setting Boundaries

(Boundary-setting skill-building)

Things I have the right to say "no" to:

- ____
- ____

Examples of how I can speak up:

- "I'm not okay with that."
- "Please stop."
- "That's not funny."
- "Don't touch me like that."

If someone ignores my 'no':

➡ I walk away.
➡ I tell someone I trust.
➡ I remind myself: *Their actions don't control my worth.*

---

5. Goal Setting Worksheet

(Confidence-building & future planning)

Short-Term Goals (next 30 days):

1. ____
2. ____

Long-Term Goals (next 6–12 months):

1. ____
2. ____

One goal I've already accomplished:

____

____

6. Grounding Techniques Page

(For managing anxiety, panic, or flashbacks)

When my brain feels out of control, I can...

5-4-3-2-1 Method

- **5 things I can see:** ______________________________
- **4 things I can touch:** ____________________________
- **3 things I can hear:** ______________________________
- **2 things I can smell:** _____________________________
- **1 thing I can taste:** ______________________________

Deep Breathing Exercise

- Inhale for 4 seconds
- Hold for 4 seconds
- Exhale for 4 seconds
- Repeat 4 times

---

7. Letter to My Future Self

(Encouragement & self-compassion practice)

Start like this:
"Dear Future Me,
Here's what I want you to remember about how far you've come…"

____

____

____

____

____

____

(Sign it with your name and keep it where only you can find it.)

www.ingramcontent.com/pod-product-compliance
Lightning Source LLC
Chambersburg PA
CBHW050604280326
41933CB00011B/1973

* 9 7 9 8 9 9 8 7 4 6 7 1 0 *